Learning
Resources
Centre

HAVERING COLLEGE

Class No.	417.7 mcg
Site	AQ 193822
Processed by	EMB
Approved by	EMB

TeXTiNg MaNuaL 4 EVeRy 1

BFF

LOL

A compilation of over 5000 Signs,
acronyms and texting symbols

Alexis McGeachy

Copyright © 2012 Alexis McGeachy
All rights reserved.

ISBN: 1467999466
ISBN 13: 9781467999465

taBLe oF CoNTeNTs

*This book does not endorse texting while driving

facTs aBouT teXTiNg

- Texting remains the most popular form of mobile communication.

- According to mashable.com, texting has surpassed e-mail, phone and face-to-face conversation as the main form of communication for 12-17-year-olds. Boys aged 14-17 send about 30 texts a day, while girls in the same age bracket send an average of 100 texts a day.

- Text messaging generated around $70bn in 2005. That's more than three times as much as all Hollywood box office returns that year.

- Texting has added a new dimension to language use.

- On Christmas Day alone in 2006, over 205m texts went out. World figures went from 17bn in 2000 to 250bn in 2001. They passed a trillion in 2005 and it was forecast to be 65bn in 2010.

- Although many texters enjoy breaking linguistic rules, they also know they need to be understood. There is no point in paying to send a message if it breaks so many rules that it ceases to be intelligible.

- Colleges and Universities use texting messages to communicate with students in case of emergencies:"Weather Alerts! No classes today due to snow storm". These institutional messages now form the majority of texts in cyberspace.

K-12 schools and colleges are better off attempting to try to come to terms with the technology rather than banned it, as many mid-state schools currently do.

EDucaToR s oPiNioN

"The reality is texting is becoming an integral part of people's lives," said Jeff Hosenfeld, the 12th-grade principal at Cumberland Valley High School, which recently amended its cell-phone policy. "Instead of denying the technology exists, we're embracing it and looking at ways to teach kids etiquette — when it's appropriate to check messages and when it's not."

IT s succiNcT

"I can text a question and get a direct answer and have a record of that reply, versus a phone call that might get voice mail and leave a rambling message," said Andy Petroski, director of Learning Technologies at Harrisburg University. "From an efficiency standpoint it certainly is beneficial."

"E-mail is not the quickest way to get a hold of somebody," said Drew Olanoff, director of community for TextPlus software. "Text messaging is good because it's instant. You know someone got it, even if they don't reply right away."

IT keePs FamiLies iN coNTacT

Many parents already know about the benefits of texting. A recent survey by TextPlus found that 66 percent of teens polled said their parents texted them during the day.

Gauge sTuDeNTs kNowLeDge

Let's say you're doing a lecture and you want to find out if the audience is "getting it." Programs such as Poll Everywhere will let you pose questions to the audience, who can then text back their responses. Their answers are then calculated live and you can see instantly what percentage of the classroom understands the material.

heLP wiTH ReaDiNg

Rather than discourage literacy, texting can actually be a boon if used correctly. Asking students, for example, to translate passages from classic literature into text-speak can help them with their language comprehension and critical thinking.

"A" teXT Message & CHaT ABBReViaTioNs

A3	Anytime, anywhere, anyplace
AA	Alcoholics Anonymous
AA	As above
AA	Ask about
AAF	As a matter of fact
AAF	As a friend
AAK	Asleep at keyboard
AAK	Alive and kicking
AAMOF	As a matter of fact
AAMOI	As a matter of interest
AAP	Always a pleasure
AAR	At any rate
AAS	Alive and smiling
AASHTA	As always, Sheldon has the answer (Bike mechanic Sheldon Brown)
AATK	Always at the keyboard
ABC	Already been chewed
ABT	About
ABT2	Meaning 'About to'
ABTA	Meaning Good-bye (signoff)
ABU	All bugged up
AC	Acceptable content
ACC	Anyone can come
ACD	ALT / CONTROL / DELETE
ACDNT	Accident (e-mail, Government)
ACE	Meaning marijuana cigarette
ACK	Acknowledge
ACPT	Accept (e-mail, Government)
ACQSTN	Acquisition (e-mail, Government)
ADAD	Another day, another dollar

ADBB	All done, bye-bye
ADD	Address
ADDY	Address
ADIH	Another day in hell
ADIP	Another day in paradise
ADMIN	Administrator
ADMINR	Administrator (Government)
ADN	Any day now
ADR	Address
AE	Area effect (online gaming)
AEAP	As early as possible
AF	April Fools
AFC	Away from computer
AFAIAA	As far as I am aware
AFAIC	As far as I am concerned
AFAIK	As far as I know
AFAIUI	As far as I understand it
AFAP	As far as possible
AFFA	Angels Forever, Forever Angels
AFJ	April Fool's joke
AFK	Away from keyboard
AFZ	Acronym Free Zone
AFPOE	A fresh pair of eyes
AH	At home
AIAMU	And I am a money's uncle
AIGHT	Alright
AIR	As I remember
AISB	As it should be
AISB	As I said before
AISI	As I see it
AITR	Adult in the room
AKA	Also known as
ALCON	All concerned
ALOL	Actually laughing out loud
AMAP	As much as possible
AMBW	All my best wishes
AML	All my love
AMOF	As a matter of fact

2

AO	Anarchy Online (online gaming)
AOC	Available on cell
AOE	Area of effect (online game)
AOM	Age of majority
AOM	Age of Mythology (online gaming)
AOTA	All of the above
AOYP	Angel on your pillow
APAC	All praise and credit
APP	Application
APP	Appreciate
AQAP	As quick (or quiet) as possible
ARE	Acronym rich environment
ASIG	And so it goes
ASAP	As soon as possible
A/S/L	Age/sex/location
ASL	Age/sex/location
ASLA	Age/sex/location/availability
AT	At your terminal
ATB	All the best
ATEOTD	At the end of the day
ATM	At the moment
ATSITS	All the stars in the sky
ATSL	Along the same line (or lines)
AWC	After awhile crocodile
AWESO	Awesome
AWOL	Away without leaving
AWOL	Absent without leave
AYDY	Are you done yet?
AYEC	At your earliest convenience
AYOR	At your own risk
AYSOS	Are you stupid or something?
AYS	Are you serious?
AYT	Are you there?
AYTMTB	And you're telling me this because
AYV	Are you vertical?
AYW	As you were
AYW	As you want / As you wish
AZN	Asian

"B" teXT Message & CHaT ABBReViaTioNs

B&	Banned
B2W	Back to work
B8	Bait (person teased or joked with, or under-aged person/teen)
B9	Boss is watching
B/F	Boyfriend
B/G	Background (personal information request)
B4	Before
B4N	Bye for now
BAG	Busting a gut
BA	Bad *a*
BAK	Back at keyboard
BAS	Big 'butt' smile
BASOR	Breathing a sigh of relief
BAU	Business as usual
BAY	Back at ya
BB	Be back
BB	Bebi / Baby / Bebe (Spanish SMS)
BBC	Big bad challenge
BBIAB	Be back in a bit
BBIAF	Be back in a few
BBIAM	Be back in a minute
BBIAS	Be back in a sec
BBL	Be back later
BBN	Bye, bye now
BBQ	Barbeque, "Ownage", shooting score/frag
BBS	Be back soon
BBT	Be back tomorrow
BC	Because
B/C	Because
BC	Be cool

BCNU	Be seeing you
BCOS	Because
BCO	Big crush on
BCOY	Big crush on you
BD	Big deal
BDAY	Birthday
B-DAY	Birthday
BDN	Big darn number
BEG	Big evil grin
BF	Boyfriend
BF	Brain fart
BFAW	Best friend at work
BF2	Battlefield 2 (online gaming)
BF	Best friend
BFF	Best friends forever
BFFL	Best friends for life
BFFLNMW	Best friends for life, no matter what
BFD	Big freaking deal
BFG	Big freaking grin
BFFN	Best friend for now
BFN	Bye for now
BG	Big grin
BGWM	Be gentle with me
BHL8	Be home late
BIB	Boss is back
BIBO	Beer in, beer out
BIC	Butt in chair
BIF	Before I forget
BIH	Burn in hell
BIL	Brother in law/Boss is listening
BION	Believe it or not
BIOYA	Blow it out your *a*
BIOYN	Blow it out your nose
BITMT	But in the meantime
BL	Belly laugh
BLNT	Better luck next time
BM	Bite me

BME	Based on my experience
BM&Y	Between me and you
BOB	Back off *buddy* or battery operate boyfriend
BN	Bad news
BOE	Meaning "bind on equip" (online gaming)
BOL	Best of luck
BOLO	Be on the look out
BOOMS	Bored out of my skull
BOP	Meaning "bind on pickup" (online gaming)
BOSMKL	Bending over smacking my knee laughing
BOT	Back on topic
BOT	Be on that
BOYF	Boyfriend
BPLM	Big person little mind
BRB	Be right back
BR	Best regards
BRBB	Be right back *babe*
BRNC	Be right back, nature calls
BRD	Bored
BRH	Be right here
BRT	Be right there
BSF	But seriously folks
BSOD	Blue screen of death
BSTS	Better safe than sorry
BT	Bite this
BT	Between technologies
BTA	But then again
BTDT	Been there, done that
BTW	By the way
BTYCL	Meaning 'Bootycall'
BUBU	Slang term for the most beautiful of women
BWL	Bursting with laughter
BYOB	Bring your own beer
BYOC	Bring your own computer
BYOP	Bring your own paint (paintball)
BYTM	Better you than me

"C" teXT Message & CHaT ABBReViaTioNs

C4N	Ciao for now
CAD	Control + Alt + Delete
CAD	Short for Canada/Canadian
CAM	Camera (SMS)
CB	Coffee break
CB	Chat break
CB	Crazy *b*
CD9	Code 9, Meaning "parents are around"
CFS	Care for secret?
CFY	Calling for you
CIAO	Good-bye (Italian word)
CICO	Coffee in, coffee out
CID	Crying in disgrace
CID	Consider it done
CLAB	Crying like a baby
CM	Call me
CMB	Call me back
CMAP	Cover my *a* partner (online gaming)
CMIIW	Correct me if I'm wrong
CMON	Come on
CNP	Continued (in) next post
COB	Close of business
COH	City of Heroes (online gaming)
COS	Because
C/P	Cross post
CP	Chat post (or continue in IM)
CR8	Create
CRAFT	Can't remember a *freaking* thing
CRB	Come right back
CRBT	Crying really big tears
CRIT	Meaning "critical hit" (online gaming)

CRZ	Crazy
CRS	Can't remember *stuff*
CSG	Chuckle, snicker, grin
CSL	Can't stop laughing
CSS	Counter-Strike Source (online gaming)
CT	Can't talk
CTC	Care to chat?
CTHU	Cracking the *heck* up
CTN	Can't talk now
CTO	Check this out
CU	See you too
CU	See you
CU2	See you
CUA	See you around
CUL	See you later
CULA	See you later alligator
CUL8R	See you later
CUMID	See you in my dreams
CURLO	See you around like a donut
CWOT	Complete waste of time
CWYL	Chat with you later
CYA	See you
CYAL8R	See you later
CYE	Check your e-mail
CYEP	Close your eyes partner (online gaming)
CYO	See you online

"D" teXT Message & CHaT ABBReViaTioNs

D2	Dedos / fingers (Spanish SMS)
D46?	Down for sex?
DA	Meaning "The"
DAoC	Dark Age of Camelot (online gaming)
DBAU	Doing business as usual
DBEYR	Don't believe everything you read
DC	Disconnect
DD	Dear (or Darling) daughter
DD	Due diligence
DEGT	Don't even go there
DFL	Dead *freaking* last (online gaming)
DGA	Don't go anywhere
DGAF	Don't give a *f**k*
DGT	Don't go there
DGTG	Don't go there, girlfriend
DH	Dear (or Darling) husband
DHU	Dinosaur hugs (used to show support)
DIIK	Darned if I know
DIKU	Do I know you?
DILLIGAF	Do I look like I give a f**k?
DILLIGAD	Do I look like I give a damn?
DIS	Did I say?
DITYID	Did I tell you I'm distressed?
DIY	Do it yourself
DKDC	Don't know, don't care
DKP	Dragon kill points (online gaming)
D/L	Download
DL	Download
DLBBB	Don't let (the) bed bugs bite
DLTBBB	Don't let the bed bugs bite

DM	Doesn't matter
DM	Direct message
DM	Do me
DM	Dungeon Master (online gaming)
DMNO	Dude Man No Offense
DMY	Don't mess yourself
DN	Down
DNC	Do not compute (meaning I do not understand)
DNR	Dinner (SMS)
DNT	Don't
d00d	Dude
DOE	Depends on experience
DP	Domestic partner
DPS	Damage per second (online gaming)
DQMOT	Don't quote me on this
DR	Didn't read
DS	Dear (or Darling) son
DTR	Define the relationship
DTRT	Do the right thing
DTS	Don't think so
DTTD	Don't touch that dial
DUPE	Duplicate
DUR	Do you remember?
DV8	Deviate
DW	Dear (or Darling) wife
DWF	Divorced white female
DWM	Divorced white male
DXNRY	Dictionary
DYNWUTB	Do you know what you are talking about?
DYFI	Did you find it?
DYFM	Dude, you fascinate me
DYJHIW	Don't you just hate it when...?

"E" teXT Message & CHaT ABBReViaTioNs

E	Ecstasy
E	Enemy (online gaming)
E1	Everyone
E123	Easy as one, two, three
E2EG	Ear to ear grin
EAK	Eating at keyboard
EBKAC	Error between keyboard and chair
ED	Erase display
EF4T	Effort
EG	Evil grin
EI	Eat it
EIP	Editing in progress
EM	Excuseme
EMA	E-mail address
EMFBI	Excuse me for butting in
EMFJI	Excuse me for jumping in
EMSG	E-mail message
ENUF	Enough
EOD	End of day
EOD	End of discussion
EOL	End of lecture
EOL	End of life
EOM	End of message
EOS	End of show
EOT	End of transmission
EQ	EverQuest (online gaming)
ERS2	Eres tz / are you (Spanish SMS)
ES	Erase screen
ESAD	Eat *S* and die!
ETA	Estimated time (of) arrival
ETA	Edited to add

EVA	Ever
EVO	Evolution
EWG	Evil wicked grin (in fun, teasing)
EWI	Emailing while intoxicated
EYC	Excitable, yet calm
EZ	Easy
EZY	Easy

"F" teXT Message & CHaT ABBReViaTioNs

F	Meaning female
F2F	Face to face
F2P	Free to play (online gaming)
FAAK	Falling asleep at keyboard
Facepalm	Used to represent the gesture of "smacking your forehead with your palm, express embarrassment or frustration
FAF	Funny as *freak*
FAQ	Frequently asked questions
FAY	F**k all you
FB	FaceBook
FBF	Fat boy food (e.g. pizza, burgers, fries)
FBFR	FaceBook friend
FBM	Fine by me
FBOW	For better or worse
FC	Fingers crossed
FC	Full card (online gaming)
FC'INGO	For crying out loud
FEITCTAJ	F**k 'em if they can't take a joke
FF	Friend x ever
FFA	Free for all (online gaming)
FFS	For f**k' sakes
FICCL	Frankly I couldn't care a less
FIF	*F**k* I'm funny
FIIK	*F**ked* if I know
FIIOOH	Forget it, I'm out of here
FIL	Father in law
FIMH	Forever in my heart
FISH	First in, still here
FITB	Fill in the blank
FML	*Freak* My Life

FOMC	Falling off my chair
FOAD	*Freak* off and die
FOAF	Friend of a friend
FOMCL	Falling off my chair laughing
FRT	For real though
FTBOMH	From the bottom of my heart
FTL	Faster than light
FTW	For the win
FU	F**k you
FUBAR	F**ked up beyond all recognition
FUBB	F**ked up beyond belief
FUD	Face up deal (online gaming)
FW	Forward
FWB	Friend with benefits
FWIW	For what it's worth
FWM	Fine with me
FYEO	For your eyes only
FYA	For your amusement
FYI	For your information

"G" teXT Message & CHaT ABBReViaTioNs

G	Grin
G	Giggle
G/F	Girlfriend
G2CU	Good to see you
G2G	Got to go
G2GICYAL8ER	Got to go I'll see you later
G2R	Got to run
G2TU	Got to tell u (you)
G4C	Going for coffee
G9	Genius
GA	Go ahead
GAC	Get a clue
GAFC	Get a f**king clue
GAL	Get a life
GAS	Got a second?
GAS	Greetings and salutations
GB	Goodbye
GBTW	Get back to work
GBU	God bless you
GD	Good
GDR	Grinning, ducking, and running
GD/R	Grinning, ducking, and running
GFI	Go for it
GF	Girl friend
GFN	Gone for now
GG	Gotta Go
GG	Good Game (online gaming)
GGA	Good game, all (online gaming)
GGE1	Good game, everyone (online gaming)
GGMSOT	Gotta get me some of that
GGOH	Gotta Get Outa Here
GGP	Got to go pee

GH	Good hand (online gaming)
GIAR	Give it a rest
GIC	Gift in crib (online gaming)
GIGO	Garbage in, garbage out
GIRL	Guy in real life
GJ	Good job
GL	Good luck
GL2U	Good luck to you (online gaming)
GLA	Good luck all (online gaming)
GL/HF	Good luck, have fun (online gaming)
GLE	Good luck everyone (online gaming)
GLE1	Good luck everyone (online gaming)
GLNG	Good luck next game (online gaming)
GMBA	Giggling my butt off
GMTA	Great minds think alike
GMV	Got my vote
GN	Good night
GNE1	Good night everyone
GNIGHT	Good night
GNITE	Good night
GNSD	Good night, sweet dreams
GOI	Get over it
GOL	Giggling out loud
GR8	Great
GRATZ	Congratulations
GRL	Girl
GRWG	Get right with God
GR&D	Grinning, running and ducking
GS	Good shot
GS	Good split (online gaming)
GT	Good try
GTFO	Get the f**k out
GTG	Got to go
GTRM	Going to read mail
GTSY	Great (or good) to see you
GUD	Good
GWHTLC	Glad we had this little chat

"H" teXT Message & CHaT ABBReViaTioNs

H	Hug
H8	Hate
H8TTU	Hate to be you
HAG1	Have a good one
HAK	Hug and kiss
HAU	How about you?
H&K	Hugs & kisses
H2CUS	Hope to see you soon
HAGN	Have a good night
HAGO	Have a good one
HAND	Have a nice day
HB	Hurry back
HB	Hug back
H-BDAY	Happy Birthday
HBU	How about you?
HF	Have fun
HFAC	Holy flipping animal crackers
H-FDAY	Happy Father's Day
HHIS	Head hanging in shame
HL	Half Life (online gaming)
HLA	Hola / hello (Spanish SMS)
H-MDAY	Happy Mother's Day
HOAS	Hold on a second
HP	Hit points / Health points (online gaming)
HRU	How are you?
HTH	Hope this helps
HUB	Head up butt
HUYA	Head up your *butt*
HV	Have
HVH	Heroic Violet Hold (online gaming)
HW	Homework

"I" teXT Message & CHaT ABBReViaTioNs

IA8	I already ate
IAAA	I am an accountant
IAAD	I am a doctor
IAAL	I am a lawyer
IAC	In any case
IAE	In any event
IANAC	I am not a crook
IANAL	I am not a lawyer
IAO	I am out (of here)
IB	I'm back
IC	I see
ICAM	I couldn't agree more
ICBW	It could be worse
ICEDI	I can't even discuss it
ICFILWU	I could fall in love with you
ICYMI	In case you missed it
IDBI	I don't believe it
IDC	I don't care
IDGAF	I don't give a f**k
IDK	I don't know
IDTS	I don't think so
IDUNNO	I don't know
IFYP	I feel your pain
IG2R	I got to run
IGHT	I got high tonight
IGN	I (I've) got nothing
IGP	I got to (go) pee
IHNI	I have no idea
IIRC	If I remember correctly
IIIO	Intel inside, idiot outside
IK	I know

IKR	I know, right?
ILBL8	I'll be late
ILU	I love you
ILUM	I love you man
ILY	I love you
IM	Instant message
IMAO	In my arrogant opinion
IMHO	In my humble opinion
IML	(in Arial font) Means I love you (a way of using the American sign language in text)
IMNSHO	In my not so humble opinion
IMO	In my opinion
IMS	I am sorry
IMSB	I am so bored
IMTM	I am the man
IMU	I miss u (you)
INAL	I'm not a lawyer
INC	Meaning "incoming" (online gaming)
IOMH	In over my head
IOW	In other words
IRL	In real life
IRMC	I rest my case
ISLY	I still love you
ITYK	I thought you knew
IUSS	If you say so
IWALU	I will always love you
IWAWO	I want a way out
IWIAM	Idiot wrapped in a moron
IYKWIM	If you know what I mean
IYO	In your opinion
IYQ	Meaning "I like you"
IYSS	If you say so

"J" teXT Message & CHaT ABBReViaTioNs

j00	You
j00r	Your
JAC	Just a second
JAM	Just a minute
JAS	Just a second
JC (J/C)	Just checking
JDI	Just do it
JFF	Just for fun
JFGI	Just f**king Google it
JIC	Just in case
JJ (J/J)	Just joking
JJA	Just joking around
JK (J/K)	Just kidding
JLMK	Just let me know
JMO	Just my opinion
JP	Just playing
JP	Jackpot (online gaming, bingo games)
JT (J/T)	Just teasing
JTLYK	Just to let you know
JV	Meaning "joint venture"
JW	Just wondering

"K" teXT Message & CHaT ABBReViaTioNs

K	Okay
KK	Knock, knock
KK	Okay, Okay!
K8T	Katie
k/b	Keyboard
KB	Keyboard
KB	Kick butt (online gaming)
KDFU	Means Cracking (K) the (D as in Da) *freak* up
KEWL	Cool
KEYA	I will key you later
KEYME	Key me when you get in
KXU	Kiss for you
KIA	Know it all
KISS	Keep it simple, stupid
KIT	Keep in touch
KMA	Kiss my *a*
KMK	Kiss my keister
KMT	Kiss my tushie
KOC	Kiss on cheek
KOL	Kiss on cheek
KOS	Kid over shoulder
KOW	Knock on wood
KOTC	Kiss on the cheek
KOTL	Kiss on the lips
KNIM	Know what I mean?
KNOW	Meaning "knowledge"
KPC	Keeping parents clueless
KS	Kill then steal (online gaming)
KSC	Kind (of) sort (of) chuckle
KT	Katie
KUTGW	Keep up the good work

"L" teXT Message & CHaT ABBReViaTioNs

L2G	Like to go?
L2G	(would) Love to go
L2K	Like to come
L8R	Later
L8RG8R	Later, gator
LBAY	Laughing back at you
LD	Later, dude
LD	Long distance
LDO	Like, duh obviously
LEMENO	Let me know
LERK	Leaving easy reach of keyboard
LFD	Left for day
LFF	Looking for group (online gaming)
LFG	Looking for guard (online gaming)
LFM	Looking for more (online gaming)
LGH	Lets get high
LH6	Lets have sex
LHSX	Lets have sex
LHM	Lord help me
LHO	Laughing head off
LI	LinkedIn
LIC	Like I care
LIK	Meaning liquor
LIMT	Laugh in my tummy
LLGB	Love, later, God bless
LLS	Laughing like *silly*
LMAO	Laughing my *a* off
LMBO	Laughing my butt off
LMFAO	Laughing my freaking a** off
LMIRL	Lets meet in real life

LMK	Let me know
LMMFAO	Laughing my mother freaking a** off
LMNK	Leave my name out
LNT	Meaning lost in translation
LOA	List of acronyms
LOL	Laughing out loud
LOL	Laugh out loud
LOL	Lots of love
LOLH	Laughing out loud hysterically
LOLO	Lots of love
LOLWTF	Laughing out loud (saying) "What the *freak*?"
LOTI	Laughing on the inside
LOTR	Lord of The Rings (online gaming)
LQTM	Laughing quietly to myself
LSHMBH	Laugh so hard my belly hurts
LSV	Language, sex and violence
LTD	Living the dream
LTLWDLS	Let's twist like we did last summer
LTNS	Long time no see
LTOD	Laptop of death
LTS	Laughing to self
LULT	Love you long time
LULZ	Slang for LOL
LVM	Left voice mail
LWOS	Laughing without smiling
LY	Love ya
LYLAS	Love you like a sis
LYLC	Love you like crazy
LYSM	Love you so much

"M" teXT Message & CHaT ABBReViaTioNs

M$	Microsoft
M8	Mate
MB	Mamma's boy
MBS	Mom behind shoulder
MC	Merry Christmas
MDIAC	My Dad is a cop
MEGO	My eyes glaze over
MEH	Meaning a "shrug" or shrugging shoulders
MEHH	Meaning a "sigh" or sighing
MEZ	Meaning "mesmerize" (online gaming)
MFI	Mad for it
MGB	May God bless
MGMT	Management
MIRL	Meet in real life
KAY	Meaning "Mmm, okay"
MLM	Meaning give the middle finger
MK	Meaning okay? (as a question)
MNC	Mother nature calls
MNSG	Mensaje (message in Spanish)
MorF	Male or female?
MOMBOY	Mamma's boy
MOO	My own opinion
MOOS	Member of the opposite sex
MOS	Mother over shoulder
MOSS	Member of same sex
MP	Mana points (online gaming)

MRT	Modified ReTweet
MSG	Message
MTF	More to follow
MTFBWU	May the force be with you
MU	Miss U (you)
MUAH	Multiple unsuccessful attempts (at/to) humor
MUSM	Miss you so much
MWAH	Meaning "kiss" (it is the sound made when kissing through the air)
MYO	Mind your own (business)
MYOB	Mind your own business

"N" teXT Message & CHaT ABBReViaTioNs

n00b	Newbie
N1	Nice one
N2M	Nothing too much
NADT	Not a darn thing
NALOPKT	Not a lot of people know that
NANA	Not now, no need
NBD	No big deal
NBFAB	No bad for a beginner (online gaming)
NC	Nice crib (online gaming)
ND	Nice double (online gaming)
NE	Any
NE1	Anyone
NFM	None for me / Not for me
NFM	Not for me
NFS	Need for Speed (online gaming)
NFS	Not for sale
NFW	No *freaking* way
NFW	Not for work
NFWS	Not for work safe
NH	Nice hand (online gaming)
NIFOC	Naked in front of computer
NIGI	Now I get it
NIMBY	Not in my back yard
NIROK	Not in reach of keyboard
NLT	No later than
NM	Nothing much
NM	Never mind
NM	Nice meld (online gaming)
NMH	Not much here
NMJC	Nothing much, just chilling
NMU	Not much, you?

NO1	No one
NOOB	Meaning someone who is bad at (online) games
NOWL	Meaning "knowledge"
NOYB	None of your business
NP	No problem
NPC	Non-playing character (online gaming)
NQT	Newly qualified teacher
NR	Nice roll (online gaming)
NRN	No response/reply necessary
NS	Nice score (online gaming)
NS	Nice split (online gaming)
NSA	No strings attached
NSFW	Not safe for work
NSISR	Not sure if spelled right
NT	Nice try
NTHING	Nothing (SMS)
NTS	Note to self
NVM	Never mind
NVR	Never
NW	No way
NWO	No way out

"O" teXT Message & CHaT ABBReViaTioNs

O4U	Only for you
O	Opponent (online gaming)
O	Meaning "hugs"
O	Over
OA	Online auctions
OATUS	On a totally unrelated subject
OB	Oh baby
OB	Oh brother
OG	Original gangster
OH	Overheard
OI	Operator indisposed
OIB	Oh, I'm back
OIC	Oh, I see
OJ	Only joking
OL	Old lady
OLL	Online love
OM	Old man
OM	Oh, my
OMAA	Oh, my aching *A* (butt)
OMDB	Over my dead body
OMFG	Oh my *freaking* God
OMG	Oh my God
OMGYG2BK	Oh my God, you got to be kidding
OMW	On my way
ONL	Online
OO	Over and out
OOC	Out of character
OOH	Out of here
OOTD	One of these days
OOTO	Out of the office

OP	On phone
ORLY	Oh really?
OT	Off topic (discussion forums)
OTB	Off to bed
OTFL	On the floor laughing
OTL	Out to lunch
OTOH	On the other hand
OTP	On the phone
OTT	Over the top
OTTOMH	Off the top of my head
OTW	Off to work
OVA	Over
OYO	On your own

"P" teXT Message & CHaT ABBReViaTioNs

P	Partner (online gaming)
P2P	Parent to parent
P2P	Peer to peer
P2P	Pay to play (online gaming)
P911	Parents coming into room alert
PAT	Meaning "patrol" (online gaming)
PAW	Parents are watching
PBOOK	Phonebook (e-mail)
PC	Player character (online gaming)
PCM	Please call me
PDA	Personal display (of) affection
PDH	Pretty darn happy
PDS	Please don't shoot
PDQ	Pretty darn quick
PEEPS	People
PFT	Pretty *freaking* tight
PIC	Picture
PIP	Peeing in pants (laughing hard)
PIR	Parents in room
PISS	Put in some sugar
PITA	Pain in the *butt*
PKMN	Pokemon (online gaming)
PL8	Plate
PLD	Played
PLMK	Please let me know
PLS	Please
PLU	People like us
PLZ	Please
PLZTLME	Please tell me
PM	Private Message
PMFI	Pardon me for interrupting

PMFJI	Pardon me for jumping in
PMSL	Pee myself laughing
POAHF	Put on a happy face
POS	Parent over shoulder
POV	Point of view
PL	People
PPU	Pending pick-up
PROLLY	Probably
PROGGY	Meaning computer program
PRON	Meaning pornography
PRT	Party
PRT	Please Retweet
PRW	People/parents are watching
PSOS	Parent standing over shoulder
PSP	Playstation Portable
PST	Please send tell (online gaming)
PTIYPASI	Put that in your pipe and smoke it
PTL	Praise the Lord
PTMM	Please tell me more
PUG	Pick up group (online gaming)
PVP	Player versus player (online gaming)
PWN	Meaning "own"
PXT	Please explain that
PU	That stinks!
PUKS	Pick up kids (SMS)
PYT	Pretty young thing
PZ	Peace
PZA	Pizza

"Q" teXT Message & CHaT ABBReViaTioNs

Q	Queue
QC	Quality control
QFE	Question for everyone
QFI	Quoted for idiocy
QFI	Quoted for irony
QIK	Quick
QL	Quit laughing
QOTD	Quote of the day
QQ (qq)	Meaning "crying eyes"
QQ	Quick question
QSL	Reply
QSO	Conversation
QT	Cutie
QTPI	Cutie pie

"R" teXT Message & CHaT ABBReViaTioNs

R8	Rate (SMS)
RBAY	Right back at you
RFN	Right *freaking* now
RHIP	Rank has its privileges
RIP	Rest in peace
RL	Real life
RLY	Really
RME	Rolling my eyes
RMLB	Read my lips baby
RMMM	Read my mail man
ROFL	Rolling on floor laughing
ROFLCOPTER	Rolling on floor laughing and spinning around
ROFLMAO	Rolling on the floor, laughing my *butt* off
ROTFL	Rolling on the floor laughing
ROTFLUTS	Rolling on the floor laughing unable to speak
RS	Runescape (online gaming)
RSN	Real soon now
RT	Roger that
RT	Retweet
RTBS	Reason to be single
RTFM	Read the *freaking* manual
RTFQ	Read the *freaking* question
RTMS	Read the manual, stupid
RTNTN	Retention (e-mail, Government)
RTRCTV	Retroactive (e-mail, Government)
RTRMT	Retirement (e-mail, Government)
RTSM	Read the stupid manual
RTWFQ	Read the whole *freaking* question
RU	Are you?
RUMOF	Are you male or female?
RUT	Are u (you) there?

RUOK	Are you okay?
RX	Regards
RW	Real world
RX	Meaning drugs or prescriptions
RYB	Read your Bible
RYO	Roll your own
RYS	Read your screen
RYS	Are you single?

"S" teXT Message & CHaT ABBReViaTioNs

S2R	Send to receiver
S2S	Sorry to say
SAL	Such a laugh
SAT	Sorry about that
SB	Should be
SB	Smiling back
SBT	Sorry 'bout that
SC	Stay cool
SDMB	Sweet dreams, my baby
SETE	Smiling Ear-to-Ear
SFAIK	So far as I know
SH	Same here
SH^	Shut up
SHID	Slapping head in disgust
SICNR	Sorry, I could not resist
SIG2R	Sorry, I got to run
SIHTH	Stupidity is hard to take
SIMYC	Sorry I missed your call
SIR	Strike it rich
SIS	Snickering in silence
SIT	Stay in touch
SK8	Skate
SK8NG	Skating
SK8R	Skater
SK8RBOI	Skater Boy
SLAP	Sounds like a plan
SMHID	Scratching my head in disbelief
SNAFU	Situation normal all fouled up
SNERT	Snot nosed egotistical rude teenager
SO	Significant other
SOAB	Son of a *B*

S'OK	Meaning It' (s) okay (ok)
SOL	Sooner or later
SOMY	Sick of me yet?
SorG	Straight or Gay?
SOS	Meaning help
SOS	Son of Sam
SOT	Short of time
SOTMG	Short of time, must go
SOWM	Someone with me
SPK	Speak (SMS)
SRSLY	Seriously
SPST	Same place, same time
SPTO	Spoke to
SQ	Square
SRY	Sorry
SS	So sorry
SSDD	Same stuff, different day
SSIF	So stupid it's funny
SSINF	So stupid it's not funny
ST&D	Stop texting and drive
STFU	Shut the *freak* up
STR8	Straight
STW	Search the Web
SUITM	See you in the morning
SUL	See you later
SUP	What's up?
SUTH	So use(d) to haters
SUX	Meanings sucks or "it sucks"
SWAK	Sent (or sealed) with a kiss
SWALK	Sealed (or sealed) with a loving kiss
SWAT	Scientific wild *butt* guess
SWL	Screaming with laughter
SWMBO	She who must be obeyed. Meaning wife or partner
SYL	See you later
SYS	See you soon
SYY	Shut your yapper

"T" teXT Message & CHaT ABBReViaTioNs

T+	Think positive
T4BU	Thanks for being you
T:)T	Think happy thoughts
TA	Thanks a lot
TAFN	That's all for now
TAM	Tomorrow a.m.
TANK	Meaning really strong
TANKED	Meaning "owned"
TANKING	Meaning "owning"
TARFU	Things Are Really *fouled* Up
TAU	Thinking about u (you)
TAUMUALU	Thinking about you miss you always love you
TBC	To be continued
TBD	To be determined
TBH	To be honest
TBL	Text back later
TC	Take care
TCB	Take care of business
TCOY	Take care of yourself
TD	Tower defense (online gaming)
TD2M	Talk dirty to me
TDTM	Talk dirty to me
TFF	Too *freaking* funny
TFS	Thanks for sharing
TFTF	Thanks for the follow
TFTI	Thanks for the invitation
TG	Thank goodness
TGIF	Thank God it's Friday
THX	Thanks
THT	Think happy thoughts

THNX	Thanks
THNQ	Thank-you (SMS)
TIA	Thanks in advance
TIAD	Tomorrow is another day
TIC	Tongue-in-cheek
TILIS	Tell it like it is
TIR	Teacher in room
TLK2UL8R	Talk to you later
TL	Too long
TMA	Take my advice
TMB	Text me back
TMB	Tweet me back
TMI	Too much information
TMOT	Trust me on this
TMTH	Too much to handle
TMWFI	Take my word for it
TNSTAAFL	There's no such thing as a free lunch
TNT	Til next time
TOJ	Tears of joy
TOS	Terms of service
TOU	Thinking of you
TOY	Thinking of you
TPM	Tomorrow p.m.
TPTB	The powers that be
TQ	Te quiero / I love you (Spanish SMS)
TSH	Tripping so hard
TSNF	That's so not fair
TSTB	The sooner, the better
TTFN	Ta ta for now
TTLY	Totally
TTTT	These things take time
TTUL	Talk to you later
TU	Thank you
TUI	Turning you in
TWSS	That's what she said
TTG	Time to go
TTYAFN	Talk to you awhile from now

TTYL	Talk to you later
TTYS	Talk to you soon
TY	Thank you
TYFC	Thank you for charity (online gaming)
TYFYC	Thank you for your comment
TYS	Told you so
TYT	Take your time
TYSO	Thank you so much
TYAFY	Thank you and *freak* you
TYVM	Thank you very much

"U" teXT Message & CHaT ABBReViaTioNs

^URS	Up yours
UCMU	You crack me up
UDI	Unidentified drinking injury
UDM	U (You) da (the) man
UDS	Ugly domestic scene
UFB	Un *freaking* believable
UFN	Until further notice
UGTBK	You've got to be kidding
UKTR	You know that's right
UL	Upload
U-L	Meaning "You will"
UNA	Use no acronyms
UN4TUN8	Unfortunate
UNBLEFBLE	Unbelievable
UNCRTN	Uncertain
UNPC	Un- (not) politically correct
UOK	(Are) You ok?
UR	You are / You're
UR2YS4ME	You are too wise for me
URA*	You are a star
URH	You are hot (U R Hot)
URSKTM	You are so kind to me
URTM	You are the man
URW	You are welcome
USBCA	Until something better comes along
USU	Usually
UT	Unreal Tournament (online gaming)
UT2L	You take too long
UTM	You tell me
UV	Unpleasant visual
UW	You're welcome

"V" teXT Message & CHaT ABBReViaTioNs

VBS	Very big smile
VEG	Very evil grin
VFF	Very freaking funny
VFM	Value for money
VGC	Very good condition
VGG	Very good game (online gaming)
VGH	Very good hand (online gaming)
VIP	Very important person
VM	Voice mail
VN	Very nice
VNH	Very nice hand (online gaming)
VRY	Very
VSC	Very soft chuckle
VSF	Very sad face
VWD	Very well done (online gaming)
VWP	Very well played (online gaming)

"W" teXT Message & CHaT ABBReViaTioNs

W@	What?
W/	With
W/B	Welcome back
W3	WWW (Web address)
W8	Wait
WAH	Working at home
WAJ	What a jerk
WAM	Wait a minute
WAN2	Want to? (SMS)
WAN2TLK	Want to talk
WAREZ	meaning pirated (illegally gained) software
WAS	Wait a second
WAS	Wild *a* guess
WAWA	Where are we at?
WAYF	Where are you from?
W/B	Write back
WB	Welcome back
WBS	Write back soon
WBU	What about you?
WC	Welcome
WC	Who cares
WCA	Who cares anyway
W/E	Whatever
W/END	Weekend
WE	Whatever
WEP	Weapon (online gaming)
WH5	Who, what, when, where, why
WIBNI	Wouldn't it be nice if
WDALYIC	Who died and left you in charge
WDYK	What do you know?
WDYT	What do you think?

WGACA	What do you think?
WIIFM	What's in it for me?
WISP	Winning is so pleasurable
WITP	What is the point?
WITW	What in the world
WIU	Wrap it up
WK	Week
WKD	Weekend
WRT	With regard to
WL	What a loser
W/O	Without
WOMBAT	Waste of money, brains and time
WOW	World of War craft (online gaming)
WRK	Work
WRU@	Where are you at?
WRUD	What are you doing?
WTB	Want to buy (online gaming)
WTF	What the f**k ?
WTFE	What the *freak* ever
WTFO	What the *freak* ?, over.
WTG	Way to go
WTGP	Want to go private (talk out of public chat area)
WTH	What the heck?
WTM	Who's the man?
WTS	Want to sell? (online gaming)
WTT	Want to trade? (online gaming)
WU	What's up?
WUCIWUG	What you see is what you get
WUF	Where are you from?
WUP	What's up?
WUW	What u (you) want?
WUU2	What are you up to?
WUZ	Meaning "was"
WWJD	What would Jesus do?
WNC	Will wonders never cease
WWYC	Write when you can
WYCM	Will you call me?

WYD	What (are) you doing?
WYGAM	When you get a minute
WYHAM	When you have a minute
WYLEI	When you least expect it
WYSIWYG	What you see is what you get
WYWH	Wish you were here

"X" teXT Message & CHaT ABBReViaTioNs

X-1-10	Meaning "Exciting"
X	Kiss
X!	Meaning "a typical woman"
XD	Meaning "really hard laugh" (where D is a smiley mouth)
XD	Meaning a "devilish smile"
XME	Excuse Me
XOXOXO	Hugs & Kisses
XLNT	Excellent
XLR8	Meaning "faster" or "going faster"
XYL	Ex-young lady, meaning wife. (amateur radio)
XYZ	Examine your zipper

"Y" teXT Message & CHaT ABBReViaTioNs

Y?	Why?
Y	Meaning Yawn
Y2K	You're too kind
YA	Your
YAA	Yet another acronym
YABA	Yet another bloody acronym
YARLY	Ya, really?
YBIC	Your brother in Christ
YBS	You'll be sorry
YCDBWYCID	You can't do business when your computer is down
YCHT	You can have them
YCLIU	You can look it up
YCMU	You crack me up
YD	Yesterday
YF	Wife
YG	Young gentleman
YGTBKM	You've got to be kidding me
YGG	You go girl
YHBT	You have been trolled
YHBW	You have been warned
YHL	You have lost
YIU	Yes, I understand
YKW	You know what
YKWYCD	You know what you can do
YL	Young lady
YMMV	Your mileage may vary
YNK	You never know
YR	Your
YR	Yeah right
YRYOCC	You're running your own cuckoo clock
YSIC	Your sister in Christ

YSYD	Yeah sure you do
YT	You there?
YTB	You're the best
YTB	Youth talk back
YTTL	You take too long
YTG	You're the greatest
YW	You're welcome
YWHNB	Yes, we have no bananas
YWHOL	Yelling "woohoo" out loud
YWSYLS	You win some, you lose some
YYSSW	Yeah, yeah, sure, sure, whatever

"Z" teXT Message & CHaT ABBReViaTioNs

Z	Zero
Z	Z's are calling (meaning going to bed/sleep)
Z	Meaning "Said"
Z%	Zoo
ZH	Sleeping Hour
ZOMG	Used in World of Warcraft to mean OMG (Oh My God)
ZOT	Zero tolerance
ZUP	Meaning "What's up?"

UNceNsoReD CHaTmaNic SigNs

- 8 = Oral sex

- 9 = Parent is watching

- 99 = Parent no longer watching

- 143 = I love you

- 182 = I hate you

- 459 = I love you

- 831 = I love you

- 1174 = Nude club

- 420 = Marijuana

- 4Q = F*** You

- ADR = Address

- AITR = Adult in the room

- ASL = Age/Sex/Location

- Banana = Penis

- BJ = Blow job

- BOB = Battery operated boyfriend

- CBF = Can't be f***ed

- CBJ = Covered blow job

- CD9 or Code 9 = Parents are around

- CYT = See you tomorrow

- DURS = Damn you're sexy

- DUM = Do you masturbate?

- DUSL = Do you scream loud?

- F2F = Face to face

- FAH = F**king A hot

- FB = F*** buddy

- FBI = Female Body Inspector

- FILF = Father I'd like to F***

- FMLTWIA = F*** Me Like The Whore I Am

- FMUTA = F*** Me Up The A**

- FO = F*** Off

- FOL = Fond of leather

- FWB = Friends with benefits

- GAP = Got a pic?

- GNOC = Get naked On cam

- GYPO = Get your pants off

- H4Y = Hot for you

- I%I = Intercourse and inebriation

- F/IB = In the front or in the back

- IIT = Is it tight?

- ILF/MD = I love female/male dominance

- IMEZRU = I am easy, are you?

- IWSN = I want sex now

- ILU = I love you

- IPN = I'm posting naked

- ITS = Intense text sex

- JAFO = Just another f***ing onlooker

- J/O = Jerking off

- JEOMK = Just ejaculated on my keyboard

- KFY or K4Y = Kiss for you

- Kitty = Vagina

- KPC = Keeping parents clueless

- KWSTA = Kiss with serious tongue action

- LB?W/C = Like bondage? Whips or chains

- LF = Let's f***

- LHOS = Let's have online sex

- LHSO = Let's have sex online

- LKITR = Little kid in the room

- LMIRL = Let's meet in real life

- LY* or LU* = Anything beginning with these are forms of I love you

- M4C = Meet for coffee

- MorF = Male or female

- MOOS = Member of the opposite sex

- MOFO = Mother f***er

- MOS = Mom over shoulder

- MILF = Mother I'd like to f***

- MIRL = Meet in real life

- MOS = Mom Over Shoulder

- MPFB = My personal f*** buddy

- MSNUW = Miniskirt no underwear

- MA = mature audience

- NIFOC = Nude in front of the computer

- NSFW = Not safe for work

- OLL = Online love

- P911 = Parent alert

- PAL = Parents are listening

- PAW = Parents are watching

- PIR = Parent in room

- PBB = Parent behind back

- PLOS = Parents looking over shoulder

- POM = Parent over my shoulder

- POS = Parent over shoulder or piece Of sh**

- PRW = Parents are watching

- PRON = Porn

- Q2C = Quick To cum

- RU/18 = Are you over 18?

- RUH = Are you horny?

- RYO = Roll your own

- S2R = Send to receive (photo)

- SorG = Straight or gay

- STM = Spank the monkey

- TAW = Teachers are watching

- TDTM = Talk dirty to me

- TTA = Tap that ass

- WOBJ = Want Online Blow J**?

- WYFM = Would you f*** me?

- WYCM = Will you call me?

- WYRN = What's your real name?

- WUF = Where you from?

MosT CommoN numBeRs & CHaRacTeRs

?	I have a question
?	I don't understand what you mean
?4U	I have a question for you
;S	Gentle warning, like "Hmm? What did you say?"
^^	Meaning "message above"
<3	Meaning "sideways heart" (love, friendship)
<3	Meaning "broken heart"
<33	Meaning "heart or love" (more 3s is a bigger heart)
@TEOTD	At the end of the day
.02	My (or your) two cents worth
1TG, 2TG	Meaning number of balls needed for win (online gaming/Bingo)
121	One-to-one (private chat initiation)
143	I love you
1432	I love you too
14AA41	One for all, and all for one
182	I hate you
19	Zero hand (online gaming)
10X	Thanks
10Q	Thank you
1CE	Once
1DR	I wonder
1NAM	One in a million
2	Meaning "to" in SMS
20	Meaning "location"
2EZ	Too easy, 2b or not 2b
2G2BT	Too good to be true, 2b@
2M2H	Too much too handle, 2bz4u = too busy for u

2MI	Too much information, 2g2bt = too good to be true
2MORO	Tomorrow, 2U2 = too u too
2NTE	Tonight
4	Short for "for" in SMS
411	Meaning "information"
404	I don't know, 4ever
459	Means I love you (ILY is 459 using keypad numbers)
4AO	For adults only
4COL	For crying out loud
4EAE	Forever and ever
4NR	Foreigner
^5	High-five
55555	Crying your eyes out (Mandarin Chinese txt msgs)
55555	Meaning Laughing (In Thai language the number 5 is pronounced 'ha'.)
6Y	Sexy
7K	Sick
831	I love you (8 letters, 3 words, 1 meaning)
86	Over
9	Parent is watching
s	Meaning "smile"
w	Meaning "wink"

EXTRa boNus,
UseFuL SymBoLs

@}.\-,. A rose
(-: Also smiling
O :-) An angel
:-|| Angry
:-o Appalled
:-x Big Kiss
:-o zz Bored
:^) Broken nose
:< Cheated
:-/ Confused
:.-(Crying
:o):o) Déjà vu
:-| Determined
8:-) Glasses on head
:-# Goatee
:.) Happy and crying
:-~) Having a cold
<3 Heart
((H)) Hug
XOXOX Hugs and kisses
:-o I.m surprised
%-} Intoxicated
:-* Kiss
:-D Laughter
:-{} Lipstick
<:-| Monk / Nun
:-| No face
:-X Not saying a word

-6% Not very clever
:-I Poker face
-:-) Punk
:-(Sad
:(Sad, without nose
:-9 Salivating
:-( ) Shocked
:-(0) Shouting
:@ Shouting
:-\ Skeptical
|-I Sleeping
:-) Smiley
:-)= Smiling with a beard
#:-) Smiling with a fur hat
:-)8 Smiling with bow tie
d:-) Smiling with cap
&:-) Smiling with curls
8-) Smiling with glasses
{:-) Smiling with hair
(:-) Smiling with helmet
C|:-) Smiling with top hat
[:-) Smiling with walkman
:) Smiling, without nose
:-? Smoking a pipe
|-O Snoring
B-) Sunglasses
B:-) Sunglasses on head
:-<> Surprised
:-v Talking
:-w Talking with two tongues
{:-) Toupee
}:-(Toupee blowing in the wind
;) Twinkle, without nose
;-) Twinkle/wink
:=) Two noses
=|:-)= Uncle Sam
:-c Unhappy

>:-(Very angry
#:o(Waking up on the wrong side of the bed
:-{) With a moustache
:-O Wow

HAVERING COLLEGE OF F & H E

193822

WITHDRAWN

14857141R00045

Printed in Great Britain
by Amazon.co.uk, Ltd.,
Marston Gate.